THE ACTOR JOURNALS

A 30-DAY JOURNAL FOR CREATIVE DEVELOPMENT, PRODUCTIVITY AND MINDFULNESS FOR DANCERS

SOPHIA MACKAY

Printed in the United Kingdom

First Printing, 2020. Revised version 2022
ISBN 978-1-913784-98-0
St. Thomas Mackay Publishing LTD
London, United Kingdom

Sophia Mackay and St.Thomas Mackay London under St.Thomas
Mackay Publishing LTD strongly recommend that you consult your
doctor before beginning any dance/vocal/exercise program. You
should be in good physical condition and be able to participate in
any activities suggested in this journal.

Sophia Mackay and St.Thomas Mackay London under St.Thomas
Mackay Publishing LTD, is not a licensed medical care provider and
represents that it has no expertise in diagnosing, examining, or
treating medical conditions of any kind, or in determining the effect
of any specific exercise on a medical condition.
If you engage in this program, you agree that you do so at your own
risk, voluntarily participating in these activities, assume all risk of
injury to yourself, and agree to release and discharge Sophia Mackay
and St.Thomas Mackay LTD from any and all claims or causes of
action, known or unknown, arising out of Sophia Mackay and
St.Thomas Mackay London under St.Thomas Mackay Publishing LTD.

www.stthomasmackay.com
@stthomasmackayldn

a letter from the author

What an honour it is to be a performer!

Building a life and career around art, creativity, exploration, and passion can be both rewarding and fulfilling, but sometimes the demands of our job can take its toll. As a musical theatre performer, I found it difficult to unwind and switch off after my shows, resulting in prolonged bouts of severe sleep deprivation, low energy and depression. I quickly realised- I wasn't the only one struggling to cope with the demands of 8 shows a week. Many of my colleagues were going through the same thing. We experienced anxiety around auditions, anxiety about the longevity of our careers, and we felt disconnected from family, friends, and a healthy work-life balance. whilst locked into a contract. The truth is that feeling disconnected and imbalanced didn't start from my first contract; for me, it started from drama school. There, the pressure to be the highest performer, to please the director and deliver perfect castings can often lead to an unfulfilled, overworked, unhealthy performer... But what if it doesn't have to be that way.

I created this journal whilst in a rut during the Global Lockdown of 2020. I was exhausted after coming off an 18-month contract with a new injury and no motivation. I so desperately wanted to feel that spark of creativity again. But this time - I wanted a way to ensure I kept myself accountable for not only the professional but the personal aspects of my life, which at the time was underdeveloped. I craved balance, and then came the inspiration for this journal!

With this journal, I intend to provide you with a safe space to reflect, plan, and prepare yourself for that which you want to invite into your life. I hope this journal helps you work through your thoughts on who you are, and where you are going, hopefully serving as a catalyst to help you get there. It is also my intention to offer some tools on how to be more productive, sharpen your skills, widen your creative palette and ultimately be the best YOU that you can be.

You may already know some things in this journal, and some may be new to you. I ask you to approach this work with an open mind and go for it! Revisit ideas you may already know and be open to new ways of working. Moreover, I challenge you to commit to consistency! Find a few bite-size daily activities from the journal you can do every day - allocate 15- 30 minutes for them each morning, and an additional 15 mins in the evening to reflect and set intentions for the following day.

This journal is about showing up for yourself, being honest with yourself and challenging yourself to evolve by releasing thoughts, feelings, and habits that no longer serve you and replacing them with those that align with your higher self. This is also about levelling up your skillset as a performer so that you can be a more productive, more creative, more impactful, happier, healthier version of YOU. Are you ready? Of course you are!

I celebrate your success, your life, and your art.

You got this! Break a Leg!
Sophia Mackay x

A GUIDE ON HOW TO USE THIS JOUNRAL

AFFIRMATIONS

Simply put, affirmations are positive statements that challenge negative thoughts and beliefs by replacing them with positive thoughts that can change how we think, behave and live. Affirmations are a powerful tool to reprogram the subconscious mind to believe positive things about yourself. They help the mind to focus on a goal, they create change in our mind and emotions and they motivate us. In addition, they make us feel more positive and energised, and they put us in a better position to make the changes we need. It is a way of returning to the truth of who we are rather than blindly accepting the opinion of who others want us to be. By repeating positive affirmative words, we can input into our minds the thoughts and ideas we want to be the foundation of our life, and in so doing cancel negative thoughts that do not serve us and restrict us from being our best selves. I recommend saying affirmations to yourself in the mirror. Start by taking 3-5 deep inhales and exhales. Then, look directly into your eyes when saying them. Why? It is said that the eyes are the gateway to the soul, and I have found something powerful happens when you can look yourself dead in the eyes and speak life into the very core of your being. Take your time and feel the words as you say them; not every affirmation given here may suit or resonate with you. That's okay. Tailor the statements by adding or omitting words and phrases as you see fit to suit your life, beliefs, and desires.

WHO AM I

This section is an extension of "Affirmations" and is a space for you to create your own positive statements about who you are and who you want to be. During the course of the next year, fill the page with statements, words and positive characteristics about yourself.

WHAT DO I WANT

Mind map where you want to be in 30 days' time, then break this down into weekly targets. Next, consider where you want to be 3 months, 6 months and one year's time, ensuring the goals and milestones you write down in the short term, align with where you want to be in the long term. Don't try to be "realistic". Allow yourself to dream and be unafraid to write down what your heart truly desires. Be creative and allow yourself to enjoy this exercise, and be open to receiving and acting upon the ideas that come to you, so you can achieve the goals you set out to accomplish.

PICK N MIX

Choose 1-2 activities per day from the Pick n Mix to complete. Mix and match hobbies with productivity tips and Singer practices that will sharpen your skill-set and elevate your artistry.

DAILY PAGES

These are divided into "Morning" and "Evening" sections. Dedicate the first 15- 30 mins of your day for the next 30 days to completing your 'Morning' section of your daily pages. Doing this will help you set the tone for the day and will also help you stay focused on important tasks. In addition, I recommend 15-20 mins right before bed for the evening section. This is where you will reflect on your day: the lessons you learnt, the wins you made and where you will set your intentions for the next day.

Do this consistently and you will surely make a few breakthroughs in the next 30 days! A part of the daily pages is the Positive Habit Tracker. You can use this to record and reinforce positive habits you want to create in your life as you make your goals a reality. These may include: making sure you drink a specific amount of water each day, regularly exercising and daily stretching/voice work. You can also use the habit tracker to release unproductive habits from your life, for example; smoking, gossiping or harmful self-talk.

Self-Reflection; Ask yourself-
What do I need to do to take my artistry to the next level? What steps do I need to take to get myself there? How can I break those steps down into bite-size daily chunks?

Now use the following pages to form a plan, and do it!

AFFIRMATION

I am an artist.
I am a powerful human being.
I am worthy of love; I am talented; I am enough; I am valuable.
I choose to show up and show out for myself daily,
giving myself what I need to be my best self.
I choose to work diligently on my craft
making choices that support my best interest.
I thank my body, my instrument, for working so hard for me, and with me.

Today my self-love is rising.
I appreciate my body.
I take care of my body by ensuring I look and feel my best and
represent myself well.
I am worthy of attracting jobs and business opportunities
where I am creatively challenged and fulfilled.
I am worthy of being in personal and professional relationships where I am appreciated
and celebrated for my contributions and for just being me.
I am worthy of receiving jobs where I am paid WELL, on time, every time in accordance
with my wants, needs and desires.

I am capable. I am unique.
No one can do what I do the way that I do it.
I don't need to judge myself for how I perform because
I am continually growing, evolving and learning.
I am open to trying new things, making mistakes,
learning from them and doing better.
Accurate practice sharpens my skills and makes me better. I have an excellent habit of
giving 100% throughout my creative practice and challenging my boundaries daily- as I
know this is how I will grow.

I am my only competition.
I don't need to compare myself to anyone because my journey is my own,
I own my path today.
I am thankful for my journey and thankful for my lessons.
I remain in excited contentment, as I enjoy where I am at,
on the way to where I am going.

I choose to remain calm and sturdy in the truth of who I am when I go to auditions,
rehearse, train and perform; knowing that I am enough.
Knowing that I have nothing to prove, knowing that the opportunities and people that are
for me- I am capable of attracting-
and so my job is to show up, and shine!
I receive my goodness with open arms.
This is my moment.
I am an artist.

WHO AM I:

FILL THIS PAGE WITH POSITIVE
CHARACTERISTICS, STATEMENTS AND
AFFIRMATIONS ABOUT YOURSELF

I am:

WHAT DO I WANT:

SHORT TERM AND LONG TERM VISION
OF WHERE YOU WANT TO BE IN
30 DAYS, IN 6 MONTHS, IN 1 YEAR AND
IN 5 YEARS TIME

personal growth

money

career and business

spiritual

health

relationships

WHAT DO I WANT:

MY 30-DAY PLANNER

WELL DONE IS BETTER THAN WELL SAID
-BENJAMIN FRANKLIN

GOALS FOR THE MONTH:

☐ _____
☐ _____
☐ _____
☐ _____

HOW WILL THE ATTAINMENT OF MY
GOALS POSITIVELY AFFECT MY LIFE:

_____
_____
_____
_____

SKILL/ HABITS TO LEARN:

I WILL SHOW MYSELF LOVE
OVER THE NEXT 30 DAYS BY:

PLAN OF ACTION/ NOTES/ MIND MAP:

CALENDAR

Monday	Tuesday	Wednesday	Thursday	Friday	Saturday	Sunday

The beginning is the most important part of the work
- Plato

NOTES

AFFIRMATION
Pick n Mix

I feel good about being me. My life matters and I am a gift to the world	The jobs I book do not define my worth	I own who I am, I own my voice, I own my artistic expression.	I have the strength to rise in the face of adversity
I am whole I am enough	I am worthy of sharing my talents, gifts and skills to the world	I work on my craft with diligence as I am committed to being my best self.	I feel the fear and do it anyway!
Everyday, in every-way- I am getting better and better and better	My self love is rising	I feel free to express myself openly, truthful and honestly	I have the power to attract money and create wealth in my life
I am worthy of love, respect and appreciation	I am a good steward of all I am gifted with	I believe in myself and my ablities	I see setbacks as stepping stones.
I give myself permission to shine	I am grateful for the gift of singing	My worth is defined by me. My worth is not defined by other peoples opinions of me	I take responsibility for my my happiness, my life and my career

PRODUCTIVITY
Pick n Mix

Do a deep clean of your bedroom	Clean your phone's photo roll and delete apps you don't use	Do a morning workout	Make a 12 month vision board
Clean up your email inbox	Wake up early	Listen to a podcast on better budgeting practices	Declutter your Kitchen
Use your commute to respond to emails, read, brainstorm and go over your daily tasks	Complete recurring tasks at the same time everyday	Sort through your income and expenses for this month	Explore a side hustle or business idea
Go to bed Early!	Spend your lunch time outdoors	Give yourself an extra-special reward today if you finish all your tasks	Drink Water!
Delegate non-productive activities	Make a shopping list for your next grocery run	Eat a healthy breakfast	Give old clothes and shoes you no longer wear to charity

ACTORS PRACTICE
Pick and Mix

Invest in a tripod, basic lighting, camera (if you don't have a phone that has a good camera) and basic plain backdrop for recording self-tapes	commit to learning an accent from a city/ borough close to you. Learn a monologue from a play that is set in that town/city.	Research a new casting director you don't know and send them your CV	Research a physical theatre style you are unfamiliar with, research and watch work from that style, attend a masterclass in that style.
Do 15 minutes of breathwork	revisit/ research an acting methodology eg: Stanislavaski, Method, Chevokhov.	Listen to an acting podcasts	Explore writing a play/short film
Record a monologue from a play/film/musical you watched in the last 6 months and post it to social media Tagging #actorjournalschallenge	Enrol in an acting class	Watch a musical and learn a new song for your songbook from that musical	Update your CV/Website/ Casting Profiles
Check in with your agents on any new jobs coming up OR send your CV to 5 perspectvie agents	Go people watching. Learn a new scene and create a character from someone you observed	Listen to a Radio drama	Book yourself in for a full body sports massage
Find a new scene and record a vocal reel	Practice Cold reading a film script	Watch a black and white movie	Do 20 mins of voice work

MORNING

Today I am grateful for:

_____

_____

I accept: _____

I deserve: _____

I love myself because: _____

Today it is my intention to: _____

_____

Important tasks:

_____

_____

_____

_____

Positive Habit Tracker

Exercise	
Water	
Meditate	
Actors Practice	

Freewriting| Brain dump| Notes:

EVENING

Daily Reflection| Todays Wins| Todays Lessons:

_____

_____

_____

_____

Tomorrow will be a great day because:

_____

_____

MORNING

Today I am grateful for:

I accept:
I deserve:
I love myself because:
Today it is my intention to:

Important tasks:

Positive Habit Tracker

Exercise

Water

Meditate

Actors Practice

Freewriting| Brain dump| Notes:

EVENING

Daily Reflection| Todays Wins| Todays Lessons:

Tomorrow will be a great day because:

MORNING

Today I am grateful for:

_____

_____

I accept: _____

I deserve: _____

I love myself because: _____

Today it is my intention to: _____

_____

Important tasks:

_____

_____

_____

_____

Positive Habit Tracker	
Exercise	☐
Water	☐
Meditate	☐
Actors Practice	☐
	☐
	☐

Freewriting| Brain dump| Notes:

EVENING

Daily Reflection| Todays Wins| Todays Lessons:

_____

_____

_____

_____

Tomorrow will be a great day because:

_____

_____

MORNING

Today I am grateful for:

_____

_____

I accept: _____

I deserve: _____

I love myself because: _____

Today it is my intention to: _____

_____

Important tasks: *Positive Habit Tracker*

_____   Exercise

_____   Water

_____   Meditate

_____   Actors Practice

_____

Freewriting| Brain dump| Notes:

EVENING

Daily Reflection| Todays Wins| Todays Lessons:

_____

_____

_____

_____

Tomorrow will be a great day because:

_____

_____

MORNING

Today I am grateful for:

_____

_____

I accept: _____

I deserve: _____

I love myself because: _____

Today it is my intention to: _____

_____

Important tasks:

_____

_____

_____

_____

Positive Habit Tracker

Exercise	☐
Water	☐
Meditate	☐
Actors Practice	☐
	☐
	☐

Freewriting| Brain dump| Notes:

EVENING

Daily Reflection| Todays Wins| Todays Lessons:

_____

_____

_____

_____

Tomorrow will be a great day because:

_____

_____

MORNING

Today I am grateful for:

_____

_____

I accept: _____

I deserve: _____

I love myself because: _____

Today it is my intention to: _____

_____

Important tasks:

_____

_____

_____

_____

Positive Habit Tracker

Exercise	☐
Water	☐
Meditate	☐
Actors Practice	☐
	☐
	☐

Freewriting| Brain dump| Notes:

EVENING

Daily Reflection| Todays Wins| Todays Lessons:

_____

_____

_____

_____

Tomorrow will be a great day because:

_____

_____

MORNING

Today I am grateful for:

_____

_____

I accept: _____

I deserve: _____

I love myself because: _____

Today it is my intention to: _____

_____

Important tasks:

_____

_____

_____

_____

_____

Positive Habit Tracker

Exercise	☐
Water	☐
Meditate	☐
Actors Practice	☐
	☐
	☐

Freewriting| Brain dump| Notes:

EVENING

Daily Reflection| Todays Wins| Todays Lessons:

_____

_____

_____

_____

Tomorrow will be a great day because:

_____

_____

MORNING

Today I am grateful for:

_____

I accept: _____

I deserve: _____

I love myself because: _____

Today it is my intention to: _____

Important tasks:

_____

_____

_____

_____

Positive Habit Tracker

Exercise	☐
Water	☐
Meditate	☐
Actors Practice	☐
	☐
	☐

Freewriting| Brain dump| Notes:

EVENING

Daily Reflection| Todays Wins| Todays Lessons:

_____

_____

_____

_____

Tomorrow will be a great day because:

_____

_____

MORNING

Today I am grateful for:

_____

_____

I accept: _____

I deserve: _____

I love myself because: _____

Today it is my intention to: _____

_____

Important tasks:

_____

_____

_____

_____

Positive Habit Tracker

Exercise	☐
Water	☐
Meditate	☐
Actors Practice	☐
	☐
	☐

Freewriting| Brain dump| Notes:

EVENING

Daily Reflection| Todays Wins| Todays Lessons:

_____

_____

_____

_____

Tomorrow will be a great day because:

_____

_____

MORNING

Today I am grateful for:

I accept:

I deserve:

I love myself because:

Today it is my intention to:

Important tasks:

Positive Habit Tracker

Exercise	
Water	
Meditate	
Actors Practice	

Freewriting| Brain dump| Notes:

EVENING

Daily Reflection| Todays Wins| Todays Lessons:

Tomorrow will be a great day because:

MORNING

Today I am grateful for:

_____

_____

I accept: _____

I deserve: _____

I love myself because: _____

Today it is my intention to: _____

Important tasks:

_____

_____

_____

_____

Positive Habit Tracker

Exercise	☐
Water	☐
Meditate	☐
Actors Practice	☐
_____	☐
_____	☐

Freewriting| Brain dump| Notes:

EVENING

Daily Reflection| Todays Wins| Todays Lessons:

_____

_____

_____

_____

Tomorrow will be a great day because:

_____

_____

MORNING

Today I am grateful for:

_____

_____

I accept: _____

I deserve: _____

I love myself because: _____

Today it is my intention to: _____

_____

Important tasks:

_____

_____

_____

_____

Positive Habit Tracker

Exercise	☐
Water	☐
Meditate	☐
Actors Practice	☐
	☐
	☐

Freewriting| Brain dump| Notes:

EVENING

Daily Reflection| Todays Wins| Todays Lessons:

_____

_____

_____

_____

Tomorrow will be a great day because:

_____

_____

MORNING

Today I am grateful for:
_____
_____

I accept: _____
I deserve: _____
I love myself because: _____
Today it is my intention to: _____
_____

Important tasks:
_____
_____
_____
_____

Positive Habit Tracker

Exercise	☐
Water	☐
Meditate	☐
Actors Practice	☐
	☐
	☐

Freewriting| Brain dump| Notes:

EVENING

Daily Reflection| Todays Wins| Todays Lessons:
_____
_____
_____
_____

Tomorrow will be a great day because:
_____
_____

MORNING

Today I am grateful for:

_____

_____

I accept: _____

I deserve: _____

I love myself because: _____

Today it is my intention to: _____

_____

Important tasks:

_____

_____

_____

_____

Positive Habit Tracker

Exercise

Water

Meditate

Actors Practice

Freewriting| Brain dump| Notes:

EVENING

Daily Reflection| Todays Wins| Todays Lessons:

_____

_____

_____

_____

Tomorrow will be a great day because:

_____

_____

MORNING

Today I am grateful for:

_____

_____

I accept: _____

I deserve: _____

I love myself because: _____

Today it is my intention to: _____

_____

Important tasks:

_____

_____

_____

_____

_____

Positive Habit Tracker

Exercise	☐
Water	☐
Meditate	☐
Actors Practice	☐
	☐
	☐

Freewriting| Brain dump| Notes:

EVENING

Daily Reflection| Todays Wins| Todays Lessons:

_____

_____

_____

_____

Tomorrow will be a great day because:

_____

_____

MORNING

Today I am grateful for:

_____

I accept: _____

I deserve: _____

I love myself because: _____

Today it is my intention to: _____

_____

Important tasks:

_____

_____

_____

_____

Positive Habit Tracker

Exercise	☐
Water	☐
Meditate	☐
Actors Practice	☐
	☐
	☐

Freewriting| Brain dump| Notes:

EVENING

Daily Reflection| Todays Wins| Todays Lessons:

_____

_____

_____

_____

Tomorrow will be a great day because:

_____

_____

RANT BELOW:

_____
_____
_____
_____
_____
_____
_____
_____
_____
_____
_____
_____
_____
_____
_____
_____
_____
_____
_____

RANT BELOW:

_____
_____
_____
_____
_____
_____
_____
_____
_____
_____
_____
_____
_____
_____
_____
_____
_____
_____
_____
_____
_____
_____
_____

RANT BELOW:

_____
_____
_____
_____
_____
_____
_____
_____
_____
_____
_____
_____
_____
_____
_____
_____
_____
_____
_____
_____
_____
_____

RANT BELOW:

_____
_____
_____
_____
_____
_____
_____
_____
_____
_____
_____
_____
_____
_____
_____
_____
_____
_____
_____
_____
_____
_____
_____

MORNING

Today I am grateful for:

_____

_____

I accept: _____

I deserve: _____

I love myself because: _____

Today it is my intention to: _____

_____

Important tasks:

_____

_____

_____

_____

Positive Habit Tracker

Exercise	☐
Water	☐
Meditate	☐
Actors Practice	☐
	☐
	☐

Freewriting| Brain dump| Notes:

EVENING

Daily Reflection| Todays Wins| Todays Lessons:

_____

_____

_____

_____

Tomorrow will be a great day because:

_____

_____

MORNING

Today I am grateful for:

I accept:

I deserve:

I love myself because:

Today it is my intention to:

Important tasks:

Positive Habit Tracker

Exercise

Water

Meditate

Actors Practice

Freewriting| Brain dump| Notes:

EVENING

Daily Reflection| Todays Wins| Todays Lessons:

Tomorrow will be a great day because:

MORNING

Today I am grateful for:

_____

_____

I accept: _____

I deserve: _____

I love myself because: _____

Today it is my intention to: _____

_____

Important tasks:

_____

_____

_____

_____

Positive Habit Tracker

Exercise	☐
Water	☐
Meditate	☐
Actors Practice	☐
	☐
	☐

Freewriting| Brain dump| Notes:

EVENING

Daily Reflection| Todays Wins| Todays Lessons:

_____

_____

_____

_____

Tomorrow will be a great day because:

_____

_____

MORNING

Today I am grateful for:

_____

_____

I accept: _____

I deserve: _____

I love myself because: _____

Today it is my intention to: _____

_____

Important tasks:

_____

_____

_____

_____

Positive Habit Tracker

Exercise	☐
Water	☐
Meditate	☐
Actors Practice	☐
	☐
	☐

Freewriting| Brain dump| Notes:

EVENING

Daily Reflection| Todays Wins| Todays Lessons:

_____

_____

_____

_____

Tomorrow will be a great day because:

_____

_____

MORNING

Today I am grateful for:

_____

_____

I accept: _____

I deserve: _____

I love myself because: _____

Today it is my intention to: _____

_____

Important tasks:

_____

_____

_____

_____

Positive Habit Tracker	
Exercise	☐
Water	☐
Meditate	☐
Actors Practice	☐
	☐
	☐

Freewriting| Brain dump| Notes:

EVENING

Daily Reflection| Todays Wins| Todays Lessons:

_____

_____

_____

_____

Tomorrow will be a great day because:

_____

_____

MORNING

Today I am grateful for:

_____

_____

I accept: _____

I deserve: _____

I love myself because: _____

Today it is my intention to: _____

_____

Important tasks:

_____

_____

_____

_____

_____

Positive Habit Tracker

Exercise	☐
Water	☐
Meditate	☐
Actors Practice	☐
	☐
	☐

Freewriting| Brain dump| Notes:

EVENING

Daily Reflection| Todays Wins| Todays Lessons:

_____

_____

_____

_____

Tomorrow will be a great day because:

_____

_____

MORNING

Today I am grateful for:

_____

I accept: _____

I deserve: _____

I love myself because: _____

Today it is my intention to: _____

_____

Important tasks:

_____

_____

_____

_____

Positive Habit Tracker	
Exercise	☐
Water	☐
Meditate	☐
Actors Practice	☐
	☐
	☐

Freewriting| Brain dump| Notes:

EVENING

Daily Reflection| Todays Wins| Todays Lessons:

_____

_____

_____

_____

Tomorrow will be a great day because:

_____

_____

MORNING

Today I am grateful for:

_____

_____

I accept: _____

I deserve: _____

I love myself because: _____

Today it is my intention to: _____

_____

Important tasks:

_____

_____

_____

_____

Positive Habit Tracker

Exercise	☐
Water	☐
Meditate	☐
Actors Practice	☐
	☐
	☐

Freewriting| Brain dump| Notes:

EVENING

Daily Reflection| Todays Wins| Todays Lessons:

_____

_____

_____

_____

Tomorrow will be a great day because:

_____

_____

MORNING

Today I am grateful for:

_____

_____

I accept: _____

I deserve: _____

I love myself because: _____

Today it is my intention to: _____

_____

Important tasks:

_____

_____

_____

_____

Positive Habit Tracker

Exercise	☐
Water	☐
Meditate	☐
Actors Practice	☐
	☐
	☐

Freewriting| Brain dump| Notes:

EVENING

Daily Reflection| Todays Wins| Todays Lessons:

_____

_____

_____

_____

Tomorrow will be a great day because:

_____

_____

MORNING

Today I am grateful for:

_____

_____

I accept: _____

I deserve: _____

I love myself because: _____

Today it is my intention to: _____

_____

Important tasks:

_____

_____

_____

_____

_____

Positive Habit Tracker	
Exercise	☐
Water	☐
Meditate	☐
Actors Practice	☐
	☐
	☐

Freewriting| Brain dump| Notes:

EVENING

Daily Reflection| Todays Wins| Todays Lessons:

_____

_____

_____

_____

Tomorrow will be a great day because:

_____

_____

MORNING

Today I am grateful for:

_____

_____

I accept: _____

I deserve: _____

I love myself because: _____

Today it is my intention to: _____

_____

Important tasks:

_____

_____

_____

_____

Positive Habit Tracker

Exercise	☐
Water	☐
Meditate	☐
Actors Practice	☐
	☐
	☐

Freewriting| Brain dump| Notes:

EVENING

Daily Reflection| Todays Wins| Todays Lessons:

_____

_____

_____

_____

Tomorrow will be a great day because:

_____

_____

MORNING

Today I am grateful for:

_____

_____

I accept: _____

I deserve: _____

I love myself because: _____

Today it is my intention to: _____

_____

Important tasks:

_____

_____

_____

_____

_____

Positive Habit Tracker

Exercise	☐
Water	☐
Meditate	☐
Actors Practice	☐
	☐
	☐

Freewriting| Brain dump| Notes:

EVENING

Daily Reflection| Todays Wins| Todays Lessons:

_____

_____

_____

_____

Tomorrow will be a great day because:

_____

_____

MORNING

Today I am grateful for:

_____

_____

I accept: _____

I deserve: _____

I love myself because: _____

Today it is my intention to: _____

_____

Important tasks:

_____

_____

_____

_____

Positive Habit Tracker	
Exercise	☐
Water	☐
Meditate	☐
Actors Practice	☐
	☐
	☐

Freewriting| Brain dump| Notes:

EVENING

Daily Reflection| Todays Wins| Todays Lessons:

_____

_____

_____

_____

Tomorrow will be a great day because:

_____

_____

MORNING

Today I am grateful for:

_____

_____

I accept: _____

I deserve: _____

I love myself because: _____

Today it is my intention to: _____

_____

Important tasks:

_____

_____

_____

_____

Positive Habit Tracker

Exercise	☐
Water	☐
Meditate	☐
Actors Practice	☐
	☐
	☐

Freewriting| Brain dump| Notes:

EVENING

Daily Reflection| Todays Wins| Todays Lessons:

_____

_____

_____

_____

Tomorrow will be a great day because:

_____

_____

MORNING

Today I am grateful for:

_____

_____

I accept: _____

I deserve: _____

I love myself because: _____

Today it is my intention to: _____

_____

Important tasks:

_____

_____

_____

_____

Positive Habit Tracker

Exercise	☐
Water	☐
Meditate	☐
Actors Practice	☐
	☐
	☐

Freewriting| Brain dump| Notes:

EVENING

Daily Reflection| Todays Wins| Todays Lessons:

_____

_____

_____

_____

Tomorrow will be a great day because:

_____

_____

MORNING

Today I am grateful for:

_____

_____

I accept: _____

I deserve: _____

I love myself because: _____

Today it is my intention to: _____

_____

Important tasks:

_____

_____

_____

_____

Positive Habit Tracker

Exercise	☐
Water	☐
Meditate	☐
Actors Practice	☐
	☐
	☐

Freewriting| Brain dump| Notes:

EVENING

Daily Reflection| Todays Wins| Todays Lessons:

_____

_____

_____

_____

Tomorrow will be a great day because:

_____

_____

MORNING

Today I am grateful for:

_____

_____

I accept: _____

I deserve: _____

I love myself because: _____

Today it is my intention to: _____

_____

Important tasks:

_____

_____

_____

_____

Positive Habit Tracker

Exercise	☐
Water	☐
Meditate	☐
Actors Practice	☐
	☐
	☐

Freewriting| Brain dump| Notes:

EVENING

Daily Reflection| Todays Wins| Todays Lessons:

_____

_____

_____

_____

Tomorrow will be a great day because:

_____

_____

MORNING

Today I am grateful for:

_____

_____

I accept: _____

I deserve: _____

I love myself because: _____

Today it is my intention to: _____

_____

Important tasks:

_____

_____

_____

_____

Positive Habit Tracker

Exercise	☐
Water	☐
Meditate	☐
Actors Practice	☐
	☐
	☐

Freewriting| Brain dump| Notes:

EVENING

Daily Reflection| Todays Wins| Todays Lessons:

_____

_____

_____

_____

Tomorrow will be a great day because:

_____

_____

MORNING

Today I am grateful for:

_____

_____

I accept: _____

I deserve: _____

I love myself because: _____

Today it is my intention to: _____

_____

Important tasks:

_____

_____

_____

_____

Positive Habit Tracker

Exercise	☐
Water	☐
Meditate	☐
Actors Practice	☐
	☐
	☐

Freewriting| Brain dump| Notes:

EVENING

Daily Reflection| Todays Wins| Todays Lessons:

_____

_____

_____

_____

Tomorrow will be a great day because:

_____

_____

MORNING

Today I am grateful for:

I accept: _____

I deserve: _____

I love myself because: _____

Today it is my intention to: _____

Important tasks:

Positive Habit Tracker

Exercise	☐
Water	☐
Meditate	☐
Actors Practice	☐
	☐
	☐

Freewriting| Brain dump| Notes:

EVENING

Daily Reflection| Todays Wins| Todays Lessons:

Tomorrow will be a great day because:

MORNING

Today I am grateful for:

_____

_____

I accept: _____

I deserve: _____

I love myself because: _____

Today it is my intention to: _____

_____

Important tasks:

_____

_____

_____

_____

Positive Habit Tracker

Exercise	☐
Water	☐
Meditate	☐
Actors Practice	☐
	☐
	☐

Freewriting| Brain dump| Notes:

EVENING

Daily Reflection| Todays Wins| Todays Lessons:

_____

_____

_____

_____

Tomorrow will be a great day because:

_____

_____

Monthly Review

PROGRESS REPORT

WINS AND LESSON FROM THIS MONTH

W

W

W

L

L

L

WHY WAS IT A WIN OR LESSONS
WHAT DID YOU LEARN & HOW CAN YOU HELP YOURSELF IMPROVE

THINGS I'VE LEARNED ABOUT MYSELF

REFELECTION

RANT BELOW:

_____
_____
_____
_____
_____
_____
_____
_____
_____
_____
_____
_____
_____
_____
_____
_____
_____
_____
_____
_____
_____
_____

RANT BELOW:

_____
_____
_____
_____
_____
_____
_____
_____
_____
_____
_____
_____
_____
_____
_____
_____
_____
_____
_____
_____
_____
_____
_____
_____
_____

RANT BELOW:

_____
_____
_____
_____
_____
_____
_____
_____
_____
_____
_____
_____
_____
_____
_____
_____
_____
_____
_____
_____
_____

RANT BELOW:

_____
_____
_____
_____
_____
_____
_____
_____
_____
_____
_____
_____
_____
_____
_____
_____
_____
_____
_____
_____
_____
_____
_____
_____

NOTES

NOTES

NOTES

NOTES

NOTES

NOTES

NOTES

NOTES

NOTES

NOTES

NOTES

NOTES

NOTES

NOTES

NOTES

Printed in Poland
by Amazon Fulfillment
Poland Sp. z o.o., Wrocław
27 December 2022

aa1234e5-3104-4477-b82c-8b8103081284R01